ETHAN ALLEN

GREEN MOUNTAIN REBEL

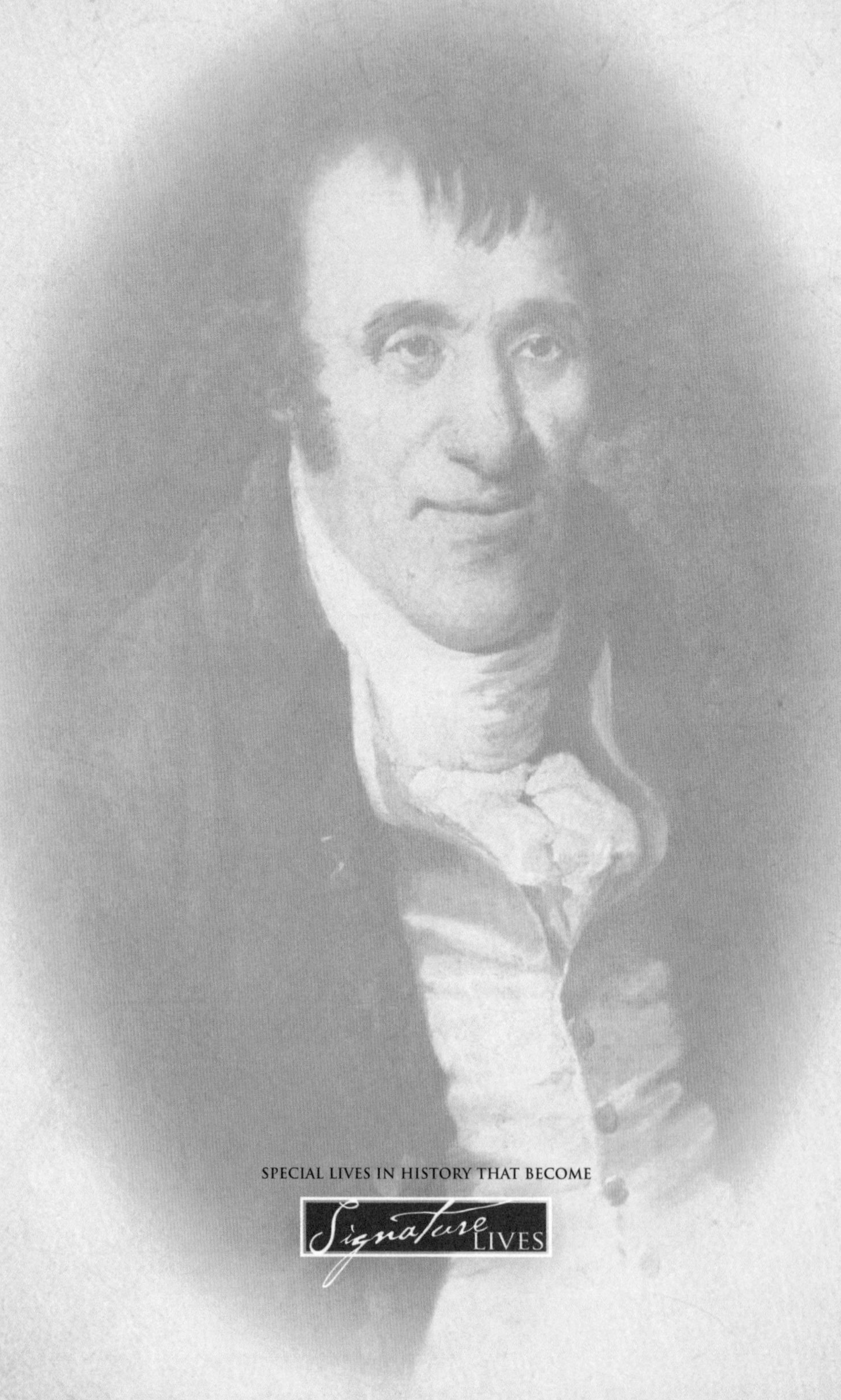

SPECIAL LIVES IN HISTORY THAT BECOME

Signature LIVES

ETHAN
ALLEN

GREEN MOUNTAIN REBEL

by Brenda Haugen

Content Adviser: Paul Searls, Ph.D.,
Visiting Assistant Professor, Department of History,
Center for Research on Vermont,
University of Vermont

Reading Adviser: Rosemary G. Palmer, Ph.D.,
Department of Literacy, College of Education,
Boise State University

COMPASS POINT BOOKS ✦ MINNEAPOLIS, MINNESOTA

Compass Point Books
3109 West 50th Street, #115
Minneapolis, MN 55410

Visit Compass Point Books on the Internet at *www.compassointbooks.com*
or e-mail your request to *custserv@compassointbooks.com.*

Editor: Jennifer VanVoorst
Lead Designer: Jaime Martens
Photo Researcher: Svetlana Zhurkina
Page Production: Heather Griffin, Bobbie Nuytten
Cartographer: XNR Productions, Inc.
Educational Consultant: Diane Smolinski

Managing Editor: Catherine Neitge
Art Director: Keith Griffin
Production Director: Keith McCormick
Creative Director: Terri Foley

To my grandma, Bernadine Kingston, who has always been a bit of a rebel
herself. BLH

Library of Congress Cataloging-in-Publication Data
Ethan Allen: Green Mountain rebel / by Brenda Haugen.
    p. cm. — (Signature lives)
  Includes bibliographical references and index.
  ISBN 0-7565-0824-X (hardcover)
  1. Allen, Ethan, 1738–1789—Juvenile literature. 2. Soldiers—United
States—Biography—Juvenile literature. 3. Vermont—Militia—
Biography—Juvenile literature. 4. Vermont—History—To 1791—Juvenile
literature. 5. Vermont—History—Revolution, 1775–1783—Campaigns—
Juvenile literature. 6. United States—History—Revolution, 1775–1783—
Campaigns—Juvenile literature. 7. Fort Ticonderoga (N.Y.)—Capture,
1775—Juvenile literature. I. Santella, Andrew. II. Title. III. Series.
E207.A4H33 2005
973.3'443'092—dc22   2004023193

Signature Lives

REVOLUTIONARY WAR ERA

The American Revolution created heroes—and traitors—
who shaped the birth of a new nation: the United States
of America. "Taxation without representation" was a serious
problem for the American colonies during the mid-1700s.
Great Britain imposed harsh taxes and didn't give the
colonists a voice in their own government. The colonists
rebelled and declared their independence from Britain—
the war was on.

Table of Contents

1 A SURPRISE ATTACK

Chapter

❦❧

On the morning of May 10, 1775, Captain William Delaplace woke to a fearsome sight. Delaplace was in command of about 50 British soldiers at Fort Ticonderoga, in the wild country of northern New York. It was a quiet post, and Delaplace spent most of his time tending his vegetable garden.

But the morning of May 10, the quiet at Fort Ticonderoga was shattered. From outside the commanding officer's quarters, Delaplace could hear the shouts of a large group of men. Something was clearly wrong.

Then came a pounding at the door. Alarmed, Delaplace threw open the door to find standing before him one of the tallest men he had ever seen. The giant was dressed in the homespun clothing of

Ethan Allen surprised the Fort Ticonderoga's British commander and forced him to surrender.

a north woods frontiersman, and he was waving a huge sword over his head. His hands were covered with cuts and scabs. Most alarming of all, he was screaming out a command for Delaplace to surrender. "Come out, you British rat!" the giant demanded.

The British captain took a moment to look around him. He could see that his soldiers, surprised

A plaque at New York's Fort Ticonderoga honors Ethan Allen's efforts in securing the fort for the American Revolutionary cause.

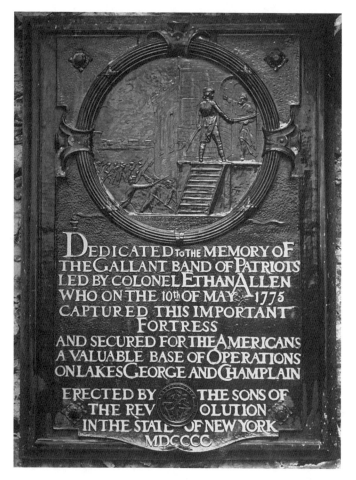

DEDICATED TO THE MEMORY OF
THE GALLANT BAND OF PATRIOTS
LED BY COLONEL ETHAN ALLEN
WHO ON THE 10th OF MAY 1775
CAPTURED THIS IMPORTANT
FORTRESS
AND SECURED FOR THE AMERICANS
A VALUABLE BASE OF OPERATIONS
ON LAKES GEORGE AND CHAMPLAIN

ERECTED BY   THE SONS OF
THE REV   OLUTION
IN THE STATE OF NEW YORK
MDCCCC

and overwhelmed by a scruffy gang of colonists, would be no help. Their weapons had been taken from them, and they were standing with their hands up, watched by a small army of frontiersmen whose rifles were pointed directly at them. Delaplace had no choice. He surrendered the fort and handed over his own sword to the giant who had roused him from his sleep. Fort Ticonderoga was now in the possession of Ethan Allen.

Ethan Allen was the leader of the Green Mountain Boys, a militia of settlers in what is now Vermont. Under Allen's command, they launched the surprise attack on Fort Ticonderoga in the earliest days of the American Revolutionary War. Without firing a shot, Allen and his Green Mountain Boys captured one of the strongest British forts in North America. It was the first time American colonists had attacked and captured a British fort, and the victory gave American patriots hope that they could defeat the mighty British army in the war to come. ௸

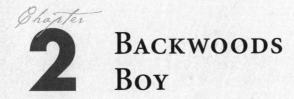

2 BACKWOODS BOY

Ethan Allen was born January 21, 1738, in Litchfield, Connecticut. He was the oldest child born to farmer Joseph Allen and his wife, Mary Baker Allen.

Before Ethan was 2 years old, his family moved west to Cornwall Township in Connecticut, a small and isolated frontier community that was just beginning to be settled. Like others in the area, the home Joseph built for his young family was made of logs and had a dirt floor. Joseph also constructed a pen to hold the few cows he had brought with him from Litchfield.

In the next 11 years, Joseph and Mary welcomed seven more children to the family—five boys and two girls. Managing a household full of children proved to be a difficult task for Mary. All of the Allen

This gristmill in present-day Vermont is much like the mills Ethan Allen traveled to in his youth.

children were very smart, but the boys in particular grew to be stubborn and bold, challenging their mother at every turn.

Ethan and his brothers and sisters grew up living the hard life of backwoods settlers in the 1700s. Ethan learned to hunt and fish at an early age. He also chopped wood for the fireplace and tended the family's crops and animals. All the children were assigned chores as soon as they were old enough to help.

Ethan learned to read when he was very young. He loved it. The first book he read was the Bible, the one book that nearly every family owned. Soon he would read whatever books he could find.

From the time he began lessons at home, Ethan showed promise as a student, and his parents hoped that he would one day attend Yale College in New Haven, Connecticut.

As a teenager, Ethan also showed great skill as a woodsman. Joseph even trusted Ethan to travel to the nearest gristmill,

As an adult, Ethan Allen knew the Bible so well that he could quote verses from it that fit just about any situation. Often he would interpret the Bible's meaning to fit his own purpose at the moment. Allen loved to use this talent to confuse his minister. During church services, Allen would often jump up and begin to argue a point his minister was trying to make. While the minister didn't appreciate the interruptions, Allen always enjoyed a good argument.

Allen grew up in a small cabin like this in the Connecticut woods.

which was 25 miles (40 kilometers) away in Woodbury. To get there, Ethan had to follow a trail through the woods. Filled with bears, wolves, rattlesnakes, and dangerous wild cats called catamounts, the woods presented many dangers. Ethan carried a gun to protect himself and other supplies to help him survive in the wilderness.

Ethan delivered sacks of grain to the gristmill to be ground into meal for his family. While he waited, he visited his friends. His uncle Remember Baker lived in Woodbury and had introduced Ethan to many of the townpeople. Ethan also enjoyed visiting with his cousin, whose name was Remember, too.

Ethan enjoyed the company of people older than himself. He understood that he could learn a great deal from their experiences, and he loved listening to their stories.

When he wasn't visiting around town, Ethan stayed around the gristmill and talked with the miller's daughter, Mary Brownson. Six years older than Ethan, Mary enjoyed flirting with the strong young man. Ethan liked Mary's attention, too.

As he grew older, Ethan needed more challenging schoolwork than his parents could provide him at home. To prepare Ethan for college, his father sent him to school in Salisbury, about 12 miles (19 km) north of Cornwall. There Ethan studied with the Reverend Jonathan Lee.

Ethan only studied in Salisbury for a short time before he was called back home. His father died unexpectedly in 1755. As the oldest son in the family, Ethan took on the responsibility of running the family farm. Just 17 years old, he needed to help provide for his mother and his seven brothers and sisters.

Ethan did not remain on the farm for long, though. A restless young man, he didn't like being tied down. He wanted action and adventure. His chance came when the Connecticut militia visited

Cornwall. On a mission to enlist new recruits, sergeants signed up 19-year-old Ethan for a local militia regiment in 1757. By now, Allen's younger brothers were old enough to handle the farm, so there was nothing to hold him back.

Great Britain and France were at war, and the French were invading Britain's American colonies from French Canada. At the time, Allen and other American colonists considered themselves loyal

France's Native American allies surprise British troops during the French and Indian War.

members of the British Empire. So Allen rushed off to defend the colonies from the French.

Allen's militia unit marched north to meet the French invasion at Fort William Henry in New York. A French force of about 7,600 was attacking the fort at the south end of Lake George. More than 2,000 British soldiers were holding the fort, but they desperately needed reinforcements. However, before Allen and the rest of the militia could reach Fort William Henry, the French forced the British to surrender. Though hungry for battle, Allen would have to wait before he would see any action.

Still, the march north was an important one for Allen. He learned that the militia used woodsmen as guides and realized that if he learned the area he could serve as a guide as well. At night, Allen listened carefully as the guides sat around campfires talking about the wild areas around Lake George and Lake Champlain. More importantly, Allen heard about their adventures in the majestic Green Mountains in what is now the state of Vermont.

The Green Mountains run through the middle of Vermont, cutting it in half from north to south. Today, thousands of people travel to Vermont each year to ski and vacation in these beautiful mountains.

The trip north marked the first time Allen saw this rugged territory. It was wild and mostly unsettled, but Allen thought it would make a good place to buy

land, settle, and raise a family. Even as he returned home to his family's farm, he vowed to return north.

Allen was drawn to land in the Green Mountains of present-day Vermont.

In 1761, an iron ore deposit was discovered in a hill near Salisbury, Connecticut. Interested in starting a mining operation, John Hazeltine of Massachusetts approached Allen about working together. They became partners in an ironworks business. An ironworks is a mill where heavy iron or steel products are produced. Hazeltine would supply most of the money, while Allen's job was to

persuade one of the hill's own-
ers to let them buy a piece
of the property. Hazelton
also built a furnace, or
forge, for turning raw
iron ore into finished
iron that could be
used for kettles and
other implements.
The business met
with success almost
immediately.

As the business grew,
the partners bought another
forge and invested in another small
piece of land where iron ore had been found.

No portrait of Ethan Allen was painted during his lifetime. Any depiction of Allen we have today was painted based on descriptions of what he looked like.

As Allen made more money, he began thinking about buying land for himself and starting a family. On June 23, 1762, he married Mary Brownson, the daughter of the Woodbury miller. Over the course of their married years, he and Mary welcomed five children to their family. As his family grew, Allen bought a nicer place in Salisbury for them to call home.

Allen was not around much to enjoy family life, however. With his brother Heman joining his business, Allen found more time to spend on other activities. He used his new free time to further educate himself. He refused to let the fact that he never went to college affect his chances for success.

Allen continued to learn by reading everything he could find. He also chose intelligent and interesting friends who would challenge his mind. One of these friends was Thomas Young. A graduate of Yale College, where Ethan had hoped to go, Young spent hours talking about science, religion, and other topics with his new friend.

Allen's old friends did not like Young. For one thing, Young was a Deist, and his religious beliefs differed from those of the strict Puritans who had settled the area. Deism is a belief system based on respect for natural laws and morality. Deists believe in God, but not in the teachings of most organized religions. For example, Deists don't believe that God interferes with the universe. To Deists, God is like a watchmaker who creates a watch, starts it, but leaves it on its own after that.

Puritans saw any beliefs outside their own as bad and frightening. When Young converted Allen to his Deist beliefs, Allen's friends were horrified.

Allen even angered town leaders by letting Young vaccinate him against the deadly disease smallpox. The new practice of vaccination was controversial. Many believed it went against the teachings of the church, so vaccination was only allowed by permission of the town selectmen, who had authority in matters of religion. Not surprisingly,

Vaccination is the process of protecting the body against disease by injecting substances that stimulate the body's immune system to produce disease-fighting substances called antibodies. These antibodies fight against particular infectious diseases and protect the person if he or she is exposed to the actual disease-causing organism. Today, vaccines protect against many deadly diseases, including smallpox, polio, influenza, and measles.

Allen never bothered to discuss his vaccination with them. Throughout his life, whenever Allen decided something, he went forward with his plan regardless of what other people thought of his decision.

The town selectmen thought they would teach Allen a lesson. They decided to arrest him for his defiance. But that turned out to be too big a task. When the selectmen arrived on Allen's doorstep, he cursed at them. He also threatened them with violence if they tried to lay a hand on him. At well over 6 feet (1.8 meters) tall, Allen towered above the other men. When his face reddened with anger, Allen could terrify just about anyone, and the selectmen were no exception. They left quickly and never bothered Allen about the vaccination issue again.

Allen's quick temper was eventually responsible for his departure from Salisbury. In 1765 Allen and his brother Herman sold their interest in a furnace to a neighbor, but there was a disagreement over the terms of the sale. After assaulting the man he felt had cheated him in the deal, Allen was forced to leave Salisbury by town leaders.

Having spent time traveling for business projects and searching for land to buy, he heard about lead being discovered in Northampton, Massachusetts. Allen decided to move his family there and begin a new mining operation. Again, however, Allen's loud mouth—and the often profane words that flew out of it—made Allen an outcast in his new community. In July 1767, Northampton's town selectmen asked him to leave.

Returning to Salisbury, Allen and his family lived above the general store owned by his brother Heman. Allen remained restless and unhappy. By 1770, he was spending most of his time in the area he had visited more than 10 years earlier when he served in the militia. This territory was called the New Hampshire Grants. ❧

Chapter 3 THE NEW HAMPSHIRE GRANTS

৻৵৵৵৶

Today, the New Hampshire Grants area makes up part of Vermont. In the 1770s, however, few people agreed on which colony owned the land. It was disputed territory, claimed by both neighboring colonies—by New Hampshire to the east and by New York to the west. It was a land of mountains and valleys, with rivers rich with fish and thick forests teeming with animals.

Government officials in New Hampshire sold plots of land in the area to new settlers. Because these new settlers owned their land under a grant from New Hampshire, they called the area the New Hampshire Grants.

There was only one problem: In New York's view, New Hampshire did not own the land it was

New Hampshire governor Benning Wentworth sold settlers land in the area known as the New Hampshire Grants.

selling, and so the settlers had no legal rights to the land they had purchased. New York's colonial government began sending surveyors to the area to plot the land's boundaries and sheriffs to enforce New York's claim to it. New York officials told the New Hampshire Grants settlers they could keep their land only if they paid another fee to New York. If they didn't pay, they would be forced off the land.

The additional fee was more than many poor farmers could afford to pay. Even if they could afford it, some simply refused to pay a second fee for land they had already bought. For the settlers, the land was not just an investment; it was their home. They had worked hard to clear trees and prepare the land for farming. They had built houses and barns and fences. Now, after all their hard work, strangers were telling them they had no right to their land. Not surprisingly, the settlers of the New Hampshire Grants refused to give up without a fight. They began to organize themselves to resist the authorities from New York and the other settlers who favored New York, whom they called "Yorkers."

Allen arrived in the New Hampshire Grants just as this struggle was beginning. He loved the towering mountains and trees, and he explored as much of the land as he could. During the winter months, he donned snowshoes and hunted deer and other wild game to store for food. At night, Allen created his own shelters, sleeping in holes hollowed in the snow or under makeshift brush houses. Wrapped in a bearskin, he kept warm on the clear, cold nights.

Because his family still remained in Connecticut, Allen didn't stay in the New Hampshire Grants for long, but he decided he wanted to make the area his home. He spent the next two summers searching for the perfect place to settle with his family.

Allen decided they would live in Bennington, in the New Hampshire Grants, and in 1769 he moved his family there. Eventually all Allen's brothers would call this area home, too. They were a family of pioneers.

England's King George II appointed Wentworth to govern New Hampshire.

Bennington was named for New Hampshire's governor, Benning Wentworth. Born in 1696 in Portsmouth, New Hampshire, he was appointed in 1741 by England's King George II as the royal governor of New Hampshire.

Wentworth loved the attention his fine clothes and shiny carriage brought him. He paid for many of these fine things with money he collected from selling land in the New Hampshire Grants.

In those days, borders between the American colonies were not well defined. Created by monarchs who lived across the sea in England and knew little about North America's geography, borders often caused disputes between neighboring colonies. When Wentworth became governor, he decided that New Hampshire's border should extend west all the way to New York.

Yet New Yorkers believed they controlled the New Hampshire Grants, extending east to the Connecticut River and New Hampshire. They based their argument on a long-standing agreement with England's King Charles II.

Governor Wentworth ignored New York's claims and began settling the New Hampshire Grants. In 1749, he collected his fees and granted a town on the west side of the Green Mountains. He even insisted the town be named after him. The community of Bennington was born.

New York did little to challenge Wentworth's

actions, but the New Hampshire governor made sure New York officials knew what he had done. Wentworth sent a letter to New York governor George Clinton with a copy of the land grant.

Clinton reacted by firing off a reply reminding Wentworth of the original agreement New York had

New York governor George Clinton found himself at odds with New Hampshire's governor regarding the New Hampshire Grants.

with King Charles II. The war of words continued until they decided to take their argument before King George II. Clinton and Wentworth called a truce: New Hampshire would refrain from giving grants for more settlements until the king made a decision on the matter.

Wentworth didn't keep his end of the bargain for long. He liked pocketing the fees he collected by selling property in the New Hampshire Grants. Soon after the truce, he granted the settlement of Halifax, followed in 1751 with grants for Marlboro and Wilmington. In 1752, he created two more towns, followed in 1753 by seven more. Meanwhile, King George II had better things to do than decide what he felt was a minor squabble between two colonies an ocean away. New York and New Hampshire still didn't have an answer.

The dispute became even more heated when Cadwallader Colden became New York's new acting governor. Since the king was ignoring the argument between New York and New Hampshire, Colden wrote to the English Board of Trade and demanded a decision be made regarding the New Hampshire Grants.

Not willing to sit idly by, Wentworth issued a proclamation stating that New York had no right to the New Hampshire Grants because it "never laid out and settled one town in that part of his Majesty's land

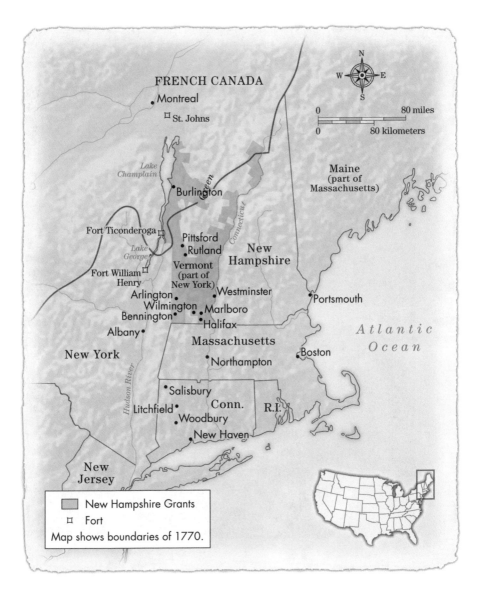

FRENCH CANADA
Montreal
St. Johns

0 — 80 miles
0 — 80 kilometers

Lake Champlain

Burlington

Maine (part of Massachusetts)

Fort Ticonderoga
Lake George
Pittsford
Rutland
Fort William Henry
Vermont (part of New York)
New Hampshire
Arlington
Wilmington
Marlboro
Westminster
Bennington
Halifax
Albany
Portsmouth
Massachusetts

New York
Northampton
Boston

Atlantic Ocean

Hudson River

Salisbury
Litchfield
Woodbury
Conn.
R.I.
New Haven

New Jersey

New Hampshire Grants
Fort
Map shows boundaries of 1770.

since she existed as a government." Although New York had granted land that overlapped settlements already granted by New Hampshire, those holding the New York grants assumed the king wouldn't dis-

The New Hampshire Grants covered much of the land that today makes up the state of Vermont.

As governor of New York, Cadwallader Colden, shown here with his grandson, tried to force a decision on the ownership of the New Hampshire Grants.

place all the people already living there, and so they never tried to settle the area.

Fourteen years passed. The issue, first presented to King George II, was then passed on to the new English king, George III. Still no decision made its way to the two angry colonies.

Governor Wentworth enjoyed the wealth that granting land brought him, and he enjoyed annoying Colden nearly as much. To further raise Colden's ire, Wentworth told his staff to treat the New Hampshire Grants as if they were a part of New Hampshire and to "deal with any persons who may presume to interrupt the inhabitants of said lands." For good measure, Wentworth also granted five new towns.

Wentworth's fun was nearing its end, though. In 1764, King George III finally decided the issue, siding with New York. But the trouble was far from over. Instead, the king's ruling would begin the conflict in earnest, and Allen would take his place right in the thick of it. ℘

4 THE GREEN MOUNTAIN BOYS

Chapter

⋐⋐∿⋑

Although King George III sided with New York, the English Board of Trade requested that the state avoid granting new titles to land already settled by New Hampshire grants. New York did not comply.

As settlers under New York grants tried to take possession of their land, the New Hampshire Grants settlers who already had made the area their home chased the New Yorkers off with their guns. Sheriffs trying to wrestle the property from previous settlers were greeted with the same welcome.

Adding to the tension and confusion, in 1770 the New York Supreme Court issued a ruling directly contradicting the English Board of Trade. The court ruled that all New Hampshire grants were invalid. Settlers already living in the New Hampshire Grants

This statue of a Green Mountain Boy stands in Rutland, Vermont.

would have to buy their property again from New York or leave immediately.

The New Hampshire Grants settlers decided to take action to protect their rightful property. They needed someone to lead them in defiance of the English king and the state of New York. Ethan Allen owned land in the New Hampshire Grants, and the New York court ruling would deprive his family of their land—and as a result, their income and stability as well. Allen's intelligence and strong personality, as well as his ties to the land, made him the perfect leader for the settlers' cause.

The 1770 case of New York against Josiah Carpenter was Allen's first real introduction to the feud. Carpenter was set to appear before the New York Supreme Court to defend his right to remain on land granted by the state of New Hampshire. This case was important because it was the first time a settler appeared in court to fight for the legality of the grants issued by New Hampshire. Ethan Allen helped Carpenter prepare his defense.

First, Allen traveled to Portsmouth, New Hampshire, to gather documents to support Carpenter's case. Governor Wentworth was more than happy to supply him with all the documents he wanted. He also suggested Allen hire attorney Jared Ingersoll to help with the case. The New Haven, Connecticut lawyer jumped at the chance to help and headed to Albany, New York with Allen.

The case went before Judge Robert Livingston in June. The result of the trial was no surprise to anyone. Judge Livingston owned 35,000 acres (14,000 hectares) granted by New York in the disputed

Judge Robert Livingston tried the case of Josiah Carpenter.

territory. To make matters worse for Carpenter, James Duane, one of the two lawyers representing New York, had also purchased lands in the New Hampshire Grants. Carpenter lost the case. Of course, with the judge and two lawyers all holding personal interests in New York's claim to the land, Carpenter's case never stood a chance.

The night after the trial ended, Allen was approached in a tavern by three men: Goldsbrow Banyar and the two attorneys who had represented New York, James Duane and John Tabor Kempe. All three owned big chunks of New York-granted land in the New Hampshire Grants. They tried to persuade Allen to talk to the settlers who had purchased land from New Hampshire. In exchange for persuading those settlers to pay the extra fee to New York, the three men promised to give Allen free land for himself. Outraged at the attempted bribe, Allen stormed out to return home to Bennington.

When settlers in the New Hampshire Grants heard that Carpenter had lost his case, they weren't surprised. They didn't expect much sympathy from the courts of New York. But they were prepared to use other means to defend their land.

The settlers of the New Hampshire Grants formed a militia called the Green Mountain Boys. Armed with hunting rifles and dressed in their homemade frontier clothes, they didn't look anything like a regular army. Nevertheless, they stood ready to defend their homes and the homes of their neighbors.

Under Ethan Allen's leadership, the Green Mountain Boys were organized into units based in Arlington, Bennington, and many of the other towns of the New Hampshire Grants territory. It wouldn't be long before their might was tested.

On July 19, 1771, New York sheriff Henry Ten Eyck came to Bennington with a large posse to force settler James Breakenridge off his land.

Early that morning, a man rode into town warning that Henry Ten Eyck was on his way with 300 men. Moving quickly, about 150 Green Mountain Boys gathered to protect Breakenridge and his farm. At the time, Allen was on another mission, so Allen's cousin Seth Warner led the group of rebels.

As the sheriff approached the Breakenridge farm, he could see his arrival had been announced. A barricade had been erected to protect the settler's door, and the cabin's log walls were filled with holes big enough for a gun barrel to fit through. In a nearby field, about 40 Green Mountain Boys stood, armed with rifles and well

Seth Warner had come to the New Hampshire Grants with his father, Dr. Benjamin Warner, long before Allen arrived. He didn't possess Allen's strong personality, but he was a good leader. He would get a chance to prove his leadership with the Green Mountain Boys.

Allen's cousin, Green Mountain Boy Seth Warner, is honored with a statue in Bennington, Vermont.

within shooting distance.

Before the sheriff and his posse reached the farmhouse, seven Green Mountain Boys stopped the group. They didn't fire a shot, but they did block the way of the sheriff and refused to budge.

Two members of the posse were allowed to

walk to the house and talk with Breakenridge. They told him they were evicting him. Breakenridge responded that his house was being protected by the town of Bennington and that he had no intention of leaving. If the sheriff and his posse wanted to use force, Breakenridge said, he was prepared to defend his property.

At that, Breakenridge raised his hand, and more Green Mountain Boys appeared from over the ridge, across from where the other rebels stood in the field. The posse representatives headed back to the sheriff to report what they had seen.

Figuring his posse outnumbered the Green Mountain Boys, the sheriff signaled his group to move toward the house. By the time he reached the home, Ten Eyck only had about 20 men left in his group. The rest had fled.

Angered by the deserters, the sheriff knew he still had a job to do. He read the eviction notice to Breakenridge and ordered him to let him in the house or he would break the door down. On one side of the sheriff, the Green Mountain Boys who were standing in the field raised their weapons. On the sheriff's other side were the men on the ridge. Ten Eyck detected movement there, too. He and his small group were trapped.

The sheriff and his remaining posse wisely decided not to fight and instead retreated to Albany,

New York. Once there, Ten Eyck told the governor that the settlers in the New Hampshire Grants were in full, armed revolt.

Ten Eyck's story was reinforced by Allen's activities at the same time. While Seth Warner organized and led the rebellion at the Breakenridge farm, Allen and some other Green Mountain Boys were harassing William Cockburn, a surveyor from New York, and his crew. Allen found Cockburn working near the New Hampshire Grant communities of Pittsford and Rutland.

Disguised as Indians, Allen and some of his Green Mountain Boys cornered Cockburn and ordered him to leave and never return. If he didn't leave, Allen warned, Cockburn would lose his head. Cockburn didn't stick around long enough to find out if Allen would truly carry out his threat.

The headquarters of the Green Mountain Boys was the Catamount Tavern in Bennington. The tavern was named for the wild mountain lions that roamed the area. Outside the tavern was a stuffed snarling catamount mounted atop a tall pole. The stuffed catamount faced west toward New York, as if it was

The Catamount Tavern stood on a hill. Never painted, the 2 1/2-story building stuck out above the trees. The lifelike stuffed mountain lion that served as the tavern's sign was terrifying. Children feared passing the sign at night.

giving a warning to anyone who might dare to enter the Green Mountains.

Inside the tavern, the Green Mountain Boys planned what they called their "wolf hunts," campaigns to scare off New York surveyors and sheriffs. When they got their hands on their enemies, the Green Mountain Boys had inventive ways of punishing them. One such unlucky fellow was Dr. Samuel Adams.

Adams had been shooting his mouth off, saying he believed New York had a right to the New Hampshire Grants and had been bullying the settlers into paying the New York fees for their land. He added that he'd shoot anyone who dared bother him about his opinion. He showed off his gun as proof.

When Allen heard what Adams said, he sent a group of Green Mountain Boys to kidnap Adams and bring him to the "judgment seat" at the Catamount. The Green Mountain Boys did as they were told. Despite Adams's earlier tough words, the Green Mountain Boys captured him without a single shot being fired.

After Adams was brought to the tavern, Allen tied Adams to a chair and led a mock trial. Adams was found guilty of defying the Green Mountain Boys by siding with the enemy. Allen sentenced the doctor to be hoisted up the Catamount sign. Using a rope, the Green Mountain Boys pulled Adams in his chair to the top of the 20-foot (6-meter) pole in front of the tavern. The Yorker stayed up there for about two hours until he admitted that he had been wrong to side with New York and to defy the Green Mountain Boys.

In their battles with the New York authorities, the Green Mountain Boys sometimes used force to threaten or punish their enemies. Although they used it infrequently, the Green Mountain Boys some-times doled out a punishment they called the "beech seal" or the "twigs of the wilderness." This punish-ment involved stripping the victim to the waist and tying him to a tree. Then, a Green Mountain Boy would beat him with a beech sapling. More often, however, the Green Mountain Boys used the threat of force to scare off their enemies. It was no wonder many outside the New Hampshire Grants regarded Allen and his militia as little more than a mob of bul-lies and outlaws.

In 1774, Ethan Allen wrote a pamphlet laying out the settlers' side of the dispute. Like many 18th cen-tury writings, the pamphlet had a lengthy title: *A Brief Narrative of the Proceedings of the Government of New York Relative to the Their Obtaining the Jurisdiction of that Large District of Land to the Westward of the Connecticut River.* The pamphlet was proof that Allen could as easily use his pen to fight for the settlers' rights as his rifle.

The Green Mountain Boys were represented by this flag.

Despite his efforts to resolve the continuing battle over land rights, New York officials still regarded Allen and his Green Mountain Boys as backwoods rebels. They believed Allen was breaking the law because he was preventing legally appointed authorities from doing their duty, and therefore he was a criminal. They put out a warrant for Allen's arrest. Ethan Allen spent the next several years as a fugitive from the law. ✎

5 WANTED MEN

❧❦❧

Allen couldn't believe what he was hearing. He roared with laughter. William Tryon, New York's new governor, was offering rewards for the capture of Allen and other leaders of the Green Mountain Boys. Allen was amused. He believed he was too smart for anyone to capture him.

Governor Tryon was known for being a tyrant. An Englishman who in 1765 had been named governor of North Carolina by the king, Tryon imposed many taxes on the citizens of North Carolina. While many citizens in North Carolina struggled to feed themselves, Tryon used their tax money to build a magnificent capital building. He used part of the new building as his home and lived there in luxury.

People from western North Carolina decided to

Ethan Allen and his Green Mountain Boys tried to get Yorker settlers to leave the New Hampshire Grants—sometimes by force.

do something about their new governor. About 4,000 of them joined together to form a group they called the Regulators. They would fight rather than pay taxes they couldn't afford. In 1771, Tryon set out to break up the Regulators. He called up the state's militia, which met about 2,000 Regulators in a battle that lasted only two hours. The rebel group was destroyed, and its leaders were hanged.

Governor Tryon called on the North Carolina militia to confront the Regulators.

The British government realized trouble would

continue if Tryon stayed in North Carolina, so they moved him to New York. Tryon immediately jumped into the land grant argument. By the end of 1772, he had already granted more than 542,000 acres (216,800 hectares), despite the fact that some of it had already been settled.

Allen and the Green Mountain Boys continued chasing away New York settlers and burning down their buildings, and Tryon took action. He offered a reward for Allen, Robert Cochran, Remember Baker, and five other high-level Green Mountain Boys.

In response, Allen offered a reward of his own. He put prices on the heads of two of New York's most respected citizens—James Duane and John Kempe, the men who had represented New York in the ill-fated Carpenter case years earlier. The poster Allen created called the two men disturbers of the public peace.

After printing posters detailing the reward, Allen distributed the posters far and wide. People in the New Hampshire Grants got a good laugh out of the poster. Imagine—two New York officials with prices on their heads!

To collect the reward, captors would have to bring Duane and Kempe to the Catamount Tavern. The reward was never collected, though. Duane and Kempe didn't test their luck and remained safely in Albany, New York.

But the rewards for Allen and his gang were no joke. Some people actually tried to collect.

On March 21, 1772, Allen's relative Remember Baker was tucked safely in his bed—or so he thought. Lurking outside was John Munro. A New Yorker and justice of the peace, Munro decided to kidnap Baker and claim the reward. He rounded up about a dozen men to help him. They waited outside in the cold and snow until they were sure Baker and his family were asleep.

On Munro's signal, the group stormed the house. Baker grabbed an ax to fend off the intruders. In the fight, a sword cut off Baker's thumb. Unable to hold his ax in his injured hand, Baker ran upstairs, kicked out some of the house's boards, and jumped outside to the ground. Baker landed in a deep drift of snow. Weak from blood loss, he was captured by Munro's band of men. They threw Baker onto their waiting sleigh and made for Albany.

The early morning ruckus roused Baker's neighbors. The neighbors alerted the Green Mountain Boys, who rushed to Baker's aid.

When the kidnappers saw the Green Mountain Boys following them, they deserted Munro, who was then forced to give up Baker. Though his hand was never the same, Baker survived.

The attack on Baker only served to make the

Green Mountain Boys angrier and more resolved to fight. They continued to harass New York settlers, and so Governor Tryon called on the New York assembly to do something to end the feud. The assembly passed the Act of Outlawry.

Known in the New Hampshire Grants as the Bloody Law, the Act of Outlawry made it illegal for three or more people to assemble in the New Hampshire Grants without lawful permission. This law now made the Green Mountain Boys' gatherings at the Catamount Tavern illegal. If a group ignored an order by a New York lawman to break up its meeting, the individuals would be thrown in jail for a year without bail. If men in the group assaulted the officer, as the Green Mountain Boys were sometimes known to do, the men would be executed. Anyone who burned down another's house, damaged crops, or pretended to be a judge—as Allen sometimes did at the tavern in "trying" cases of New Yorkers—also would be executed.

In addition, the Act of Outlawry raised the rewards for the capture of Allen and Remember Baker. The rewards offered on some of the other

> *Remember Baker returned to the Green Mountain Boys and was involved in some of their most famous encounters, including the capture of Ticonderoga in 1775. Baker was killed by Native Americans while on a scouting mission on the Richelieu River in August 1775.*

Green Mountain Boys were increased as well. The act went on to say that those with prices on their heads were required by law to surrender. If the wanted men failed to do so within 70 days, they would be judged guilty without a trial and sentenced to die.

As always, Allen and the Green Mountain Boys ignored the new law. In fact, Allen even wrote a letter to Governor Tryon daring the governor to come and get him.

The Act of Outlawry didn't slow down Allen at all. He overpowered two New York sheriff's deputies and took them to a nearby settler's home. Allen locked the deputies in separate rooms. In the evening, he talked to each deputy individually. Allen told them, one at a time, that each was a good man who was simply led astray by the other. Allen promised each man that he would be set free in the morning if he promised to go back to New York and never return. But Allen said that he would hang the other deputy.

That night, Allen crept up to a tree on a nearby hill. He rigged up a dummy one of his friends had made. From a distance, the dummy looked like a real man hanging from a tree limb.

In the morning, Allen showed up where the deputies were being held captive. He took one deputy outside and set him free. After seeing the figure hanging from the distant tree, the deputy couldn't leave fast enough. Allen did the same with the other deputy. It wasn't until later, when the two deputies met in New York, that they realized Allen had made fools of them.

Many tried to capture Allen and his friends, but no one was successful. The reward was eventually forgotten as other events in the colonies became more important. Soon the rebel leader and his Green Mountain Boys would be called upon to help their country fight an even bigger battle. ❧

6 MORE DEFIANCE

Chapter

⤴︎⤵︎

In 1772 and 1773, Allen worked in Salisbury, Connecticut. Along with three of his brothers and Remember Baker, Allen founded the Onion River Company. The men had pooled their money and bought as much land as they could in the New Hampshire Grants—more than 45,000 acres (18,000 hectares).

The Onion River Company ran an advertisement in the *Connecticut Courant*. The ad detailed the beautiful area along the falls of the Onion River where the company held its property and offered the land for sale to settlers. The land would be sold under New Hampshire titles, not New York titles.

Enchanted by the beautiful description of the area, some of Salisbury's leading residents decided

American Minutemen fought the British at the battles of Lexington and Concord, the first of the Revolutionary War.

Thomas Chittenden, who bought land from Allen's Onion River Company, would later work with Allen's brother Ira to create the Vermont Constitution.

to try their luck in the new land. Among those buying property from the Onion River Company was Thomas Chittenden, who later became Vermont's first governor when it gained statehood.

Not content to sell property to settlers who would then be faced with Yorker harrassment, the Onion River Company protected its investment by building Fort Frederick and stocking it with guns and ammunition. In addition, Allen and the Green Mountain Boys continued to chase off Yorkers. Sometimes the group assaulted settlers from New York. Other times they destroyed property, burned homes, and ruined crops.

While Allen's men pretty much controlled the New Hampshire Grants west of the Green Mountains, New York had established two counties—complete with courts—on the east. In March 1775, the court in Westminster was ready to bring several cases to trial. All involved evicting settlers who had New Hampshire grants.

Before they were to go to court, the settlers

pleaded with the judge to dismiss their cases. When he pledged to push forward with the trial, about 100 settlers armed with clubs traveled to Westminster. On March 13, the settlers quickly took control of the courthouse.

Told they would be thrown out once the sheriff and his men arrived, many of the settlers left the courthouse. A few, however, stayed behind, unwilling to give up the fight.

That night, Sheriff William Paterson and a group of about 50 men demanded they be allowed in the courthouse. When the remaining settlers refused to open the door, the sheriff broke it down. In the fight that followed, one settler was killed and others were injured. Another settler would later die from his injuries.

The sheriff's actions only served to make the rest of the settlers more angry. Within hours, an armed mob of more than 400 formed in the town. Afraid for his life, the judge postponed the day's court session.

By the time news of the event reached the Green Mountain Boys, the fight was over, and there was nothing they could do.

The conflict between the settlers and the Yorkers continued until a greater conflict arose. On April 19, 1775, Massachusetts colonists clashed with British soldiers at Lexington and Concord, marking

Battles in the Revolutionary War took place throughout the colonies.

the start of the Revolutionary War.

To Allen and the other Green Mountain Boys, independence from Great Britain was another cause

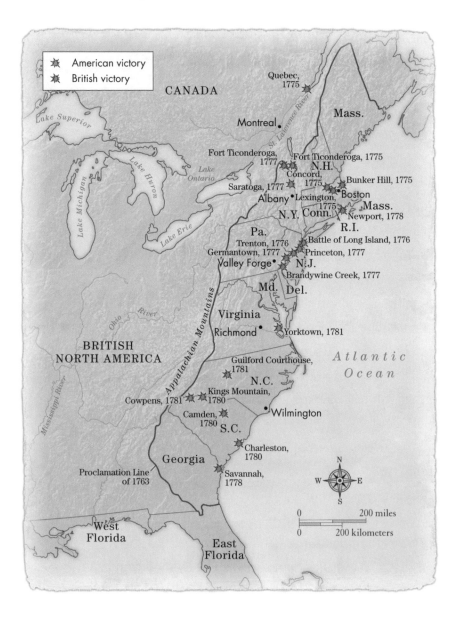

for which they were willing to fight. Allen quickly took up what he considered to be a noble fight. "Ever since I arrived to a state of manhood … I have felt a sincere passion for liberty," Allen later wrote.

In the early days of the war, the Continental Congress rushed to organize the Continental Army and appointed George Washington as commander. At the same time, individual colonies were organizing their own military forces and planning their own campaigns. A group of colonial leaders from Connecticut knew of Allen's reputation and recruited him for a special assignment. They wanted him to attack Fort Ticonderoga, the British post in New York on the south end of Lake Champlain. ✑

7 TAKING FORT TICONDEROGA

❧⌇❧

With its thick stone walls, Fort Ticonderoga was considered one of the strongest forts in North America. Its location on the western shore of the 100-mile (160-kilometer) long Lake Champlain made it vitally important. Lake Champlain and the Hudson River formed a natural invasion route that could carry a British army from Canada south into the heart of the American colonies. However, no army could travel down Lake Champlain without first passing Fort Ticonderoga.

American patriots yearned to take Fort Ticonderoga, not only for its choice position, but also because the fort held a large supply of heavy cannons and ammunition, which were badly needed by the new patriot armies. Allen knew that the New

In his assault on Fort Ticonderoga, Allen and his Green Mountain Boys surprised the fort's commander and other British soldiers.

Hampshire Grants settlers would need to occupy Fort Ticonderoga in order to preserve their claims on the land, and he agreed to the assault the colonial leaders had proposed.

But Allen wasn't the only one who had plans to assault the fort. The Massachusetts Committee of Safety asked an officer named Benedict Arnold to lead his own attack. Arnold later became infamous as a traitor to the American cause, but in the early days of the war, he proved himself a courageous and skilled officer.

When Arnold and Allen learned of each other's plans, each one expected the other to step aside. Eventually, the leaders agreed to share command of a force of about 150 colonists. Most of this small army was made up of Green Mountain Boys, and there was no doubt in their minds about who was in charge. They took their orders from Ethan Allen.

As his little army marched north toward Fort Ticonderoga, Allen sent scouts ahead to learn what

Benedict Arnold would later work against the American cause in the Revolutionary War.

they could about the British forces there. The scouts informed Allen that only about 50 British soldiers were stationed at the fort.

When Allen and his troops arrived at Lake Champlain, however, they faced a problem. Fort Ticonderoga stood on the opposite shore, so Allen had to find boats to move his soldiers across the lake. He found only two boats, which had room for only about 80 men. Before sunrise on May 10, 1775, they quietly rowed across the lake and then marched toward the fort.

Their attack on Fort Ticonderoga completely surprised the British at the fort. Allen's troops entered the fort through a gap in the outer walls and quickly charged into the heart of the fort. Allen and his soldiers surprised a sleeping sentry who was supposed to be standing guard. When the sentry opened his eyes and saw a giant in a big green coat, he tried to fire his weapon. Luckily for Allen, the musket failed to work properly.

The sentry dropped the musket and took off running, yelling at the top of his lungs. Allen calmly but quickly forged ahead, his troops following him into the fort.

The surprise attack worked so well that they captured the fort without firing a single shot. Not a single soldier on either side was killed.

Allen walked to the officers' quarters and

demanded to speak to the British commander. He was met by a British lieutenant who had been startled from his sleep and was still trying to get dressed. Stammering and wearing no pants, the officer asked Allen in whose name he dared to attack the fort. According to legend, Allen replied, "In the name of the great Jehovah and the Continental Congress."

Allen soon found the commanding officer, Captain Delaplace, who officially surrendered the fort. The British captain ordered his troops to parade before Allen's force in a traditional show of surrender. From the time Allen encountered the sentry to the time Captain Delaplace surrendered, less than an hour had passed.

The work of the Green Mountain Boys was not finished, however. As soon as Fort Ticonderoga was under his control, Allen sent a smaller force led by Seth Warner to capture the British post at Crown Point a few miles to the north. In all, Allen's men captured about 60 British prisoners that day and seized boats, food, gunpowder, and other supplies. But the most important prize of all was inside Fort Ticonderoga. There the Green Mountain Boys found about 200 cannons—just the

The British recaptured Fort Ticonderoga in 1777 but abandoned it again three years later. The fort was rebuilt in 1908 and became a museum.

thing the patriot forces needed most in the early days of the war. Before long, American forces moved the Ticonderoga cannons south to Boston, where they would help General George Washington in his fight with the British.

Cannons and powder captured at Fort Ticonderoga were later transported to Boston and used in the city's defense.

The taking of Fort Ticonderoga was a stunning turn of events. Ethan Allen and his Green Mountain Boys had captured a key British fort and important supplies, all without the loss of a single soldier. In the early days of the war, many people wondered about the ability of the American colonists to defeat the mighty British army. News of the victory spread and boosted confidence in the American cause. 🙟

8 DISASTER AT MONTREAL

∽◦✦◦∾

The capture of Fort Ticonderoga had been so easy that Allen was eager for more battles and more victories.

Plans were in the works for an invasion of Canada, which was then a British possession, and Allen wanted to be a part of it. He believed that with a small force of Green Mountain Boys, he could capture the British-held city of Montreal, one of the largest cities in Canada.

The biggest obstacle to reaching Montreal was the British fort at St. Johns, Canada. Benedict Arnold raced there and overtook the fort before Allen's arrival. Allen continued on, though, planning to hold the fort and possibly go on to capture Montreal on his own. While Allen and his men

During his assault on Montreal, Allen and his men were attacked by British forces.

remained at the fort, however, British reinforcements arrived and chased them out. Defeated,
Allen led his group back to Crown Point, but he
didn't forget about Montreal.

Determined to take an active part in the war
effort, Allen wrote to the New York Provincial
Congress and offered his services. The congressmen
had once been his enemies, but now that the
colonies were fighting a war, Allen was willing to let
go of the past and fight for the liberty of the
American colonies. In his letter, Allen asked the congress to provide money and the authority for him to
raise a military regiment. With New York's help,
Allen believed he and the Green Mountain Boys
could not only take Montreal but conquer all
of Canada.

While waiting for a reply from the New York congress, Allen and Seth Warner were asked to talk to
the Continental Congress on the very same issue.
After talking with Allen, the Continental Congress
became convinced that an invasion of Canada
should be attempted. However, members of
Congress did not believe Allen was the right person
to lead the fight.

The Continental Congress urged the New York
Provincial Congress to talk with General Philip
Schuyler. It further suggested Schuyler make
use of the Green Mountain Boys along with his

regular soldiers.

Upon hearing this, Allen and Warner went to the New York Congress and offered the services of the Green Mountain Boys. Showing up in front of the New York government was a bold move considering both still had prices on their heads. Some

Ethan Allen hoped General Philip Schuyler, shown here, would support his planned invasion of Montreal.

lawmakers grumbled about whether it was appropriate to let known criminals speak before them, but eventually Allen and Warner were admitted to the congress's chamber.

Allen described his plan to the lawmakers. He said he would serve as colonel and lead the Green Mountain Boys, with Warner being second-in-command of the group. General Schuyler would command the larger group, which included the regular army and the Green Mountain Boys.

Allen was happy to have his feuding days with New York behind him. His good mood wouldn't last long, though. Congress decreed that the Committees of Safety in the New Hampshire Grants should choose the leadership of the regiment made up of Green Mountain Boys. The Committees of Safety chose Warner as their leader. Other officer positions were filled as well, two of them by Allen's brothers, but none were offered to Ethan Allen. He was heartbroken.

Bold, independent, and sometimes rude, Allen may have been offensive to some of the older men on the town safety committees. His Deist religious beliefs may have kept the committee from offering him a position also. However, Allen believed, if the Green Mountain Boys had been allowed to choose, his own name would have topped the list of officers.

For the most part, Allen kept quiet about the officer choices. He hoped the Continental Congress

would correct what he believed was a huge error. In
a letter to his friend Governor Jonathan Trumbull of
Connecticut, Allen said,

> *Notwithstanding my zeal and success in
> my country's cause, the old farmers on the
> New Hampshire Grants, who do not
> incline to go to war, have met in a com-
> mittee meeting, and in their nomination
> of officers for the regiment of Green
> Mountain Boys who are quickly to be
> raised, have wholly omitted me, but as
> the commissions will come
> from the Continental Congress,
> I am hopeful they will
> remember me, as I desire to
> remain in the service. ... I
> find myself in the favor of
> the officers of the army and
> the young Green Mountain
> Boys. How the old men came
> to reject me, I cannot con-
> ceive, inasmuch as I saved
> them from the encroachments
> of New York.*

Jonathan Trumbull
was the only colonial
governor to hold his
position both before
and after the
Revolutionary War.
His son, Jonathan Jr.,
also became a governor
of Connecticut.

When the Continental Congress made no
changes in the officers chosen, Allen went to
General Schuyler himself and offered to help.
Schuyler found a mission for Allen.

Montreal and its surrounding area were filled
with French Canadian settlers who resented living

under British rule. The settlers stubbornly hung onto their language and customs. They also were angered by laws passed by the British Parliament that they believed infringed on their rights. The French Canadians would make natural allies for the Americans in their war against the British. Allen was given the job of recruiting them to join the American invasion force.

While most of the French Canadians Allen encountered were friendly to the American cause, they did not want to join the battle right away. They wanted to see if the Americans stood a chance of winning against the British before they would commit to any help. When Allen reported this to the general, Schuyler sent him out again. This time Allen found more success. In a letter to another general, Allen said:

> You may rely on it that I shall join you in about three days with 500 or more volunteers. I could raise one or two thousand in a week's time, but will first visit the army with a less number, and if necessary will go out again.

However, Allen did not return to his base with any troops. He had decided that the job of recruiting French Canadians troops was not important enough for him. He wanted to command the troops. Going beyond his orders from the general, Allen assembled a group of 100 soldiers and decided to launch his own assault on Montreal.

Allen had planned to be aided in his assault of Montreal by his friend Colonel John Brown. A native of Massachusetts, Brown, too, had been sent on a

This letter was written by Allen in 1775, the year he captured Fort Ticonderoga and tried to invade Montreal.

recruiting mission to Canada. The two devised a plan to take the city themselves. Allen and his recruits would attack Montreal from the north, while Brown and his men would assault the city from the south.

Allen and his troops began marching toward Montreal on September 25, 1775. He had hoped to once more catch the British by surprise, but this time the British were ready for him. Before they could attack, Allen and his men were met by a force of about 300 British soldiers and their Native American

This image shows Montreal as it looked around the time of Allen's assault.

allies. Under fire, many of Allen's men turned and fled. Badly outnumbered, Allen and the remains of his army were captured.

Colonel John Brown, who was to attack from the south, never showed up. Brown never discussed the incident after the fact, so historians don't know why.

Allen later wrote about the incident:

> *I thought to have enrolled my name in the list of illustrious American heroes, but was nipped in the bud. ... I had no chance to fly. We were [captured] by Canadians, with a number of English who lived in the town, and some Indians.*

Allen's grand plans for taking Montreal had turned into a disaster, and he was now a prisoner of the British. ᕲ

9 HELD CAPTIVE

❦

Allen's defeat at Montreal began a two-and-a-half-year ordeal as a British prisoner. Immediately after the battle, Allen and his soldiers were marched through the streets of Montreal by the British. Crowds who had gathered to watch jeered at the intruders.

No one attracted more attention than Allen. His fame had already spread in the days after the capture of Fort Ticonderoga. British officers were delighted to have captured such a well-known American leader. They told Allen that he would hang for his part in the rebellion against Great Britain. They didn't hang him, but he was treated harshly as a prisoner. Much of the next two years of his life was spent in horrible conditions and under cruel

This late 18th century illustration shows a suspected American spy captured by the British.

treatment aboard a series of British ships.

During the American Revolution, the British housed thousands of American prisoners in ships used as floating prisons. In some cases, as many as a thousand prisoners might be crammed into the largest ships. They often lived in filthy conditions, eating, sleeping, and relieving themselves in the same small spaces.

Under such conditions, diseases spread quickly. Many prisoners grew weak and came down with yellow fever, smallpox, and other diseases. So many prisoners died from disease, starvation, and violence that each morning the British jailers on some ships would have to collect the prisoners who had died overnight. "Rebels, turn out your dead," they called.

At first, British officers and government leaders were not quite sure what to do with Ethan Allen. Some favored hanging him as a traitor, but others feared that if they were to hang such a well-known American leader, the Americans would respond by hanging British prisoners.

As they debated Allen's fate, the British moved him from ship to ship. Finally they decided to send

A. Bobbett

Allen was kept chained and below deck while on the British prison ship.

him to England aboard the warship *Adamant*. Allen and 33 other prisoners were locked in a wooden cage below the deck of the ship for 40 days as the *Adamant* made its way across the Atlantic Ocean.

Locked in their dark and wretched jail, the prisoners struggled to survive. What little food the British gave the prisoners was often rotten.

The sailors quickly realized Allen's hot temper was easy to trigger. With Allen securely chained, the sailors taunted him mercilessly. With his wrists in handcuffs and leg irons weighing 30 pounds (14 kilograms) attached to his ankles, Allen could hardly move. They laughed when Allen turned red and began swearing and pulling at his chains.

When the ship finally landed in Falmouth, England, the prisoners were a sorry-looking group. Their clothes were in tatters. They were filthy, unshaven, and thin from hunger and disease. Allen fared no better. He had lost a great deal of weight, and his health was failing.

A crowd gathered along the route to the prison at Pendennis Castle. People wanted to see the giant who captured Fort Ticonderoga.

Life in Pendennis Castle was not much better than being imprisoned at sea. Allen slept on a bunk with only straw for a mattress. Lice covered his body. Yet Allen continued to be a big attraction. People wanted to see the famous Ethan Allen and paid prison guards to have the honor of doing so. Allen was like an animal in a zoo.

Allen stayed in Pendennis Castle just three weeks, but his suffering was not over. On January 8, 1776, Allen was put back on a British warship. The *Solebay* was part of a fleet of 45 British ships heading for North America. The ships formed an expedition to invade the Carolinas, led by Lord Cornwallis. But before it began its journey across the Atlantic

Ocean, the *Solebay* stopped in Cork, Ireland, to stock up on provisions. It was in Cork that Allen experienced the first kind treatment he had enjoyed in a long time.

Allen spent three weeks imprisoned in England's Pendennis Castle.

The Irish recognized the big man who talked about American freedom. Ireland also had been harshly ruled by England. The Irish sympathized with the American cause and with Allen. They gave him clothes, food, and wine. The ship's captain quickly took away the food and wine, but allowed Allen to keep the clothes. Allen was grateful even for that.

On February 12, 1776, the *Solebay* began its voyage across the Atlantic Ocean. Again Allen was confined below deck. Constantly cold and hungry, he fell ill. Despite his weak condition, Allen was thrilled to catch sight of his home country again. On May 3, the *Solebay* anchored off Cape Fear, North Carolina. Soon, though, Allen and the other prisoners were moved to yet another ship—the *Mercury*—and traveled to Halifax, Novia Scotia.

The cruel captain of the *Mercury* told Allen he would be hanged once they reached Nova Scotia. That wasn't true, but Allen didn't know that. He grew weaker and more ill as he spent his days imprisoned below deck in the dark with little food. The captain refused to let the ship's doctor help any of the prisoners, and Allen was no exception.

If Allen thought life couldn't get worse, he was wrong. In Halifax, the prisoners were transferred to another boat waiting in the harbor. Though he was not to be hanged, Allen and the other prisoners continued to slowly starve.

Desperate, Allen managed to persuade one of his guards to help him and the rest of the prisoners by taking a letter to the governor of Halifax, Admiral Marriot Arbuthnot. In the letter, Allen described the wretched conditions the prisoners were forced to live under.

When the letter reached Arbuthnot, he took immediate action. He sent one of his officers and a surgeon to investigate Allen's claims. The men returned to Arbuthnot and confirmed that what Allen had said was true. Appalled, the governor ordered that sick prisoners be taken to the hospital and the others to be brought to the jail in Halifax. They would still be locked up, but at least they would be treated like human beings.

Halifax governor Marriot Arbuthnot worked to improve Allen's conditions.

On October 12, 1776, Allen and the other prisoners boarded the *Lark*, which was bound for New York. To Allen's surprise and relief, the captain treated the prisoners well and the trip was bearable. By the end of November, the prisoners were taken ashore. Allen was granted parole but was ordered not to leave New York City.

With all the suffering he had been through, Allen

was just a shell of a man compared to the strong, muscled hulk he had once been. Allen later wrote: "My constitution was almost worn out by such a long and barbarous captivity. The enemy gave out that I was crazy."

Even with his limited freedom, Allen quickly regained his health. He also regained his fighting spirit. Always a rebel, Allen tried to leave New York City, a violation of his parole. On August 25, 1777, Allen was thrown in jail once again.

Allen's brothers Heman and Levi worked hard to get him out of jail. After much pressure, they were able to persuade Generals George Washington and Philip Schuyler to help win Allen's release. On May 3, 1778, they succeeded in arranging an exchange of prisoners. The British agreed to release Allen and other American prisoners in exchange for the freedom of a number of British officers being held by the Americans.

Ethan Allen had been a prisoner of the British for nearly three years. Having spent much of this time in the hull of a prison ship, he was delighted to finally be free—and on dry land. Allen later wrote, "In a

Revolutionary War General George Washington helped free Ethan Allen from British captivity.

transport of joy, I landed on liberty ground, and as I advanced into the country, received the acclamation of the people." ✺

10 THE HERO'S RETURN

❦

Allen's first stop as a free man was Valley Forge, Pennsylvania. He traveled 100 miles (161 kilometers) to visit General Washington and thank him for his help in winning his freedom. Washington came away from the meeting impressed with the giant from the New Hampshire Grants.

"There is an original something in him that commands admiration; and his long captivity and suffering have only served to increase, if possible, his enthusiastic zeal," Washington wrote.

Congress rewarded Allen by making him a colonel in the Continental Army, his first appointment as an officer. His attacks on Fort Ticonderoga and Montreal had been undertaken as an ordinary civilian.

Late in 1778, Allen returned to the New

While Allen was imprisoned in England, the Green Mountain Boys helped American forces defeat the British at Saratoga.

Hampshire Grants and was greeted with a joyful welcome. In Bennington, cannons on the village square fired a salute to the returned hero.

Allen soon discovered that a great deal had happened at home while he was gone. While he was in prison, his Green Mountain Boys continued to fight against the British, scoring a major victory at the Battle of Bennington in 1777. That victory helped drive British forces from the area, and the New

The Green Mountain Boys clashed with British forces again in the Battle of Bennington.

Hampshire Grants, now called Vermont, declared itself an independent republic in 1777.

Even though Vermont had declared itself independent, it was still threatened by opposing forces on all sides. Thousands of British soldiers positioned in Canada threatened to invade Vermont at any time, and there were still some officials in New York who insisted that the area was part of New York.

In 1779, Allen was elected head of the Vermont militia. In this role, Allen traveled to Philadelphia several times to meet with the Continental Congress, hoping to persuade them to make Vermont the 14th state.

That same year, Allen published *A Narrative of Colonel Ethan Allen's Captivity*, the story of the ordeals he endured during his years as a prisoner of the British. The narrative covered the period of his captivity from May 1775 until his release in May 1778. It first appeared as a magazine serial but was soon reprinted as a book. The book revealed the inhumane conditions on British prison ships and motivated the American colonists in their fight

Allen's A Narrative of Colonel Ethan Allen's Captivity covers more than just the period of his captivity. It details his military career and includes information about the revolutionary efforts of the colonials. The book has been republished many times and is available in many libraries.

After his release from prison, Allen was given the rank of lieutenant colonel.

against the British.

Allen's book also made him even more famous, and he became a legend in his own time. Dozens of incredible stories about him were told. Some said he could run so fast, he could catch a deer. Others said Allen could bend nails with his teeth.

Allen hoped his fame and influence would help further Vermont's goal of becoming the 14th state. Congress was not ready to take that step, however. Members of Congress did not want to anger New York and New Hampshire leaders, who still made claims on the Vermont territory.

Allen feared that without statehood Vermont would be swallowed up by one of the states that surrounded it. In the final years of the war, he began secret negotiations with the British. The British offered to make a separate peace settlement if Vermont would become a British province. Allen did not agree or disagree immediately but continued to negotiate with the British.

Ever since, historians have debated about Allen's actions. Did he give up on the American cause over the issue of Vermont statehood and decide to go over to the British side? Or was he only pretending to negotiate, hoping to delay a British invasion and occupation of Vermont? Whatever the truth, the war ended in 1783 with the British safely out of Vermont. ❧

ETHAN ALLEN

11 THE FINAL YEARS

ೕೕ❀ೕೕ

Allen's wife Mary died in 1783. The next year he married a young woman named Frances Montresor Buchanan, and the two soon moved to a farm near Burlington, Vermont. There Allen built a new home on several hundred acres of land near the Onion River, now called the Winooski River. There the second Mrs. Allen gave birth to two sons and a daughter.

In 1784, Allen published a book that angered many American religious leaders, and made him the target of severe criticism. The book was titled *Reason, the Only Oracle of Man*, but many people simply called it "Allen's Bible." In it, Allen criticized the teachings of many of the world's organized religions, and he claimed that God was not found in churches but instead was present everywhere in the natural world. Allen's book was widely read, even in Europe, and many consider it to be the first book by an American writer to attack organized religion.

The winter of 1789 was unusually harsh in Vermont. And yet despite the cold weather, there were chores to be done and animals to be fed. On a cold and wintry day in February, Allen set out in a farm wagon to cross frozen Lake Champlain. He planned to buy a load of hay for his livestock.

Fighting his way back home through the cold and wind, Allen suffered a stroke and had to be carried home by one of his farm workers. He died the next day, on February 12, 1789. Allen was 51 years old. His death came as a shock to all the Vermonters who thought that their hero was indestructible.

Allen was given a soldier's funeral. The Green Mountain Boys formed an escort for his coffin. Drums rolled as the snow slowly fell. Members of the Vermont militia fired their guns in salute as the coffin was lowered into its grave in Burlington's Greenmount Cemetery. A fitting phrase is etched in his tombstone: "His Spirit Tried The Mercies of His God, In Whom Alone He Believed and Strongly Trusted.".

Just two years later, in 1791,

According to legend, Ethan Allen believed that he would be reincarnated, or brought back to life, as a white horse.

Ethan Allen's brother Ira and Thomas Chittenden worked to create the Vermont Constitution.

Vermont entered the Union as the 14th state. Ethan Allen, the rebel who had fought for American independence and had worked so hard to protect Vermont, did not live to see it happen. Yet he is remembered as a hero of Vermont and of the Revolution. This giant of a man with his larger-than-life spirit left an indelible mark on the the land and country he loved so much. ✒

ALLEN'S LIFE

1739

Allen family moves
to Cornwall,
Connecticut

1738

Born January 21
in Litchfield,
Connecticut

1735

1740

1738

Englishman John
Wesley and his
brother Charles found
the Methodist church

1740

The War of Austrian
Succession, or King
George's War, breaks
out in Europe

WORLD EVENTS

1755

Ends schooling to return home after the death of his father

1757

Joins British militia during the French and Indian War

1755

1759

The British Museum opens in London

ALLEN'S LIFE

1771

Organizes Green Mountain Boys

1761

Launches ironworks business with John Hazeltine

1762

Marries Mary Brownson

1765

1764

James Hargreaves creates the spinning jenny, a mechanical spinning wheel

1762

Catherine the Great becomes empress of Russia and rules for 34 years

WORLD EVENTS

1775

Leads successful
assault of Fort
Ticonderoga;
captured by British
during attack on
Montreal

1778

Released from British
prison ship as part of
a prisoner exchange;
Allen petitions
Congress for
Vermont's statehood

1776

Scottish economist
Adam Smith publishes
*The Wealth of
Nations*, heralding
the beginning of
modern economics

1778

British explorer
Captain James Cook
explores the
Hawaiian Islands

ALLEN'S LIFE

1784

Marries Frances
Montresor; publishes
*Reason, the Only
Oracle of Man*

1783

American
Revolutionary War
ends; Mary Allen dies

1780

1783

The first manned
hot air balloon
flight is made in
Paris, France, by the
Montgolfier brothers

WORLD EVENTS

1789

Dies February 12

1791

Vermont becomes 14th state

1790

1789

The French Revolution begins with the storming of the Bastille prison in Paris

1791

Austrian composer Wolfgang Amadeus Mozart dies

DATE OF BIRTH: January 21, 1738

BIRTHPLACE: Litchfield, Connecticut

FATHER: Joseph Allen

MOTHER: Mary Baker Allen

EDUCATION: Several years of instruction under a local minister in Salisbury, Connecticut

FIRST SPOUSE: Mary Brownson (1732–1783)

DATE OF MARRIAGE: 1762

CHILDREN: Loraine (1763–1783)
Joseph (1765–1777)
Lucy (1768–1842)
Mary Ann (1772–1790)
Pamela (1779–1809)

SECOND SPOUSE: Frances Montresor (1760–1834)

DATE OF MARRIAGE: 1784

CHILDREN: Fanny (1784–1819)
Hannibal (1787–1813)
Ethan (1787–1855)

DATE OF DEATH: February 12, 1789

PLACE OF BURIAL: Burlington, Vermont

In the Library

Aronson, Virginia. *Ethan Allen: Revolutionary Hero*. Philadelphia: Chelsea House, 2001.

Hahn, Michael T. *Ethan Allen: A Life of Adventure*. Shelburne, Vt.: New England Press, 1994.

Raabe, Emily. *Ethan Allen: The Green Mountain Boys and Vermont's Path to Statehood*. New York: PowerPlus Books, 2002.

Stein, R. Conrad. *Ethan Allen and the Green Mountain Boys*. New York: Children's Press, 2003.

ON THE WEB

For more information on *Ethan Allen,* use FactHound to track down Web sites related to this book.

1. Go to *www.facthound.com*
2. Type in this book ID: 075650824X
3. Click on the *Fetch It* button.

FactHound will find the best Web sites for you!

HISTORIC SITES

Ethan Allen Homestead
1 Ethan Allen Homestead, Suite 2
Burlington, VT 05401
802/865-4556
To tour Ethan Allen's home and see exhibits related to his life and times

Fort Ticonderoga National Historic Landmark
Fort Road
Ticonderoga, NY 12883
518/585-2821
To see the restored military fortress and tour a military history museum

assembly
a group of people who make laws

evicting
forcing someone to move out of a home, building, or occupied land

feud
a bitter quarrel between two people, families, or groups that lasts for a long time

grant
something given by the government or an organization for a special purpose

gristmill
a mill for grinding grain

militia
a group of citizens who volunteer to perform military duties during times of emergency

monarchs
rulers, such as kings and queens, who often inherit their positions

ordeal
a very difficult or painful experience

ore
a mineral collected by mining that contains some valuable substance

pamphlet
a short printed publication

parole
the release of a prisoner before his or her full sentence has been served

posse
a group of citizens gathered by authorities to help in law enforcement

Puritans
members of a reform movement who wished to
purify the Church of England from within and not
separate from it; they favored simple church services and a strict moral code

rebels
people who fight against a government or another
authority

regiment
a military unit

sentry
a soldier standing guard at a fort or a camp

surveyors
people whose job it is to measure the shape, size,
and position of a piece of land

titles
documents that show legal ownership

truce
a temporary agreement to stop fighting

tyrant
someone who rules others in a cruel or unjust way

warrant
a legal document calling on authorities to carry out
the law

Chapter 1

Page 10, line 5: Edwin P. Hoyt. *The Damndest Yankees: Ethan Allen and His Clan.* Brattleboro, Vt.: The Stephen Greene Press, 1976, p. 34.

Chapter 3

Page 30, line 27: Clifford Lindsey Alderman. *Gathering Storm: The Story of the Green Mountain Boys.* New York: J. Messner, 1970, p. 34.

Page 33, line 7: Ibid., p. 35.

Chapter 6

Page 59, line 3: *The Damndest Yankees: Ethan Allen and His Clan*, p. 36.

Chapter 7

Page 64, line 6: Ibid., p. 41.

Chapter 8

Page 71, line 4: *Gathering Storm: The Story of the Green Mountain Boys*, p. 104.

Page 72, line 18: Ibid., p. 109.

Page 75, line 8: *The Damndest Yankees: Ethan Allen and His Clan*, p. 55.

Chapter 9

Page 84, line 4: Red Reeder. *Bold Leaders of the American Revolution.* Boston: Little, Brown, 1973, pp. 16-17.

Page 84, line 28: Ibid., p. 18.

Chapter 10

Page 87, line 7: Ibid.

Alderman, Clifford Lindsey. *Gathering Storm: The Story of the Green Mountain Boys*. New York: J. Messner, 1970.

Brown, Slater. *Ethan Allen and the Green Mountain Boys*. New York: Random House, 1956.

Holbrook, Stewart H. *Ethan Allen*. Portland, Ore: Binfords and Mort, 1958.

Hoyt, Edwin P. *The Damndest Yankees: Ethan Allen and His Clan*. Brattleboro, Vt.: The Stephen Greene Press, 1976.

Jellison, Charles A. *Ethan Allen: Frontier Rebel*. Syracuse, N.Y.: Syracuse University Press, 1969.

Reeder, Red. *Bold Leaders of the American Revolution*. Boston: Little, Brown, 1973.

Brenda Haugen is the author and editor of many books, most of them for children. A graduate of the University of North Dakota in Grand Forks, Brenda lives in North Dakota with her family.

Image Credits

Lombard Antiquarian Maps & Prints, cover (top), 4–5; Library of Congress, cover (bottom), 2, 46, 62, 96 (bottom), 97 (bottom), 99 (bottom), 100, 101 (bottom); Stock Montage, 8, 99 (top); John Phillips/Time Life Pictures/Getty Images, 10; Jim Zuckerman/Corbis, 12; MPI/Getty Images, 15, 17, 69, 96 (top), 97 (top); James P. Blair/Corbis, 19; Bettmann/Corbis, 20, 27; North Wind Picture Archives, 24, 34, 48, 56, 60, 65, 74, 79, 90; Francis G. Mayer/Corbis, 29, 37; *Cadwallader Colden and His Grandson Warren De Lancey* by Matthew Pratt, The Metropolitan Museum of Art, Morris K. Jesup Fund, 1969, accession no. 69.76, photo by the Metropolitan Museum of Art, 32; Lee Snider/Photo Images/Corbis, 40; Robin V. Burr/George Merrick Troop 7 Historic Flag Collection, 45, 98 (top); Art Resource, N.Y., 54; Courtesy of the National Museum of the U.S. Army, Army Art Collection, 66, 86; John Phillips/Time Life Pictures/Getty Images, 73; Mary Evans Picture Library, 76; Art Directors, 81; Courtesy FCIT, 83; Réunion des Musées Nationaux/Art Resource, N.Y., 85; Corbis, 88; Architect of the Capitol, 93, 101 (top left); The Archival Image, 95, 101 (top right); Hulton/Archive by Getty Images, 98 (bottom).